JOHN SUMMERS & SYLVIA CORTHORN

La choquante vérité d'un avocat d'Ottawa et d'une juge de la Cour supérieure de l'Ontario

Peter Tremblay

Agora Éditeurs™
Ottawa, Canada

John Summers & Sylvia Corthorn: La choquante vérité d'un avocat d'Ottawa et d'une juge de la Cour supérieure de l'Ontario

© 2021 par Peter Tremblay

Tous droits réservés. Aucune partie de ce livre ne peut être reproduite, stockée dans un système de récupération ou transmise sous quelque forme que ce soit ou par quelque moyen que ce soit, électronique ou mécanique, y compris la photocopie, l'enregistrement ou autre sans le consentement écrit d'Agora Cosmopolite.

Des précautions ont été prises pour retracer la propriété / la source de tout matériel académique ou autre référence contenu dans ce texte. L'éditeur acceptera avec gratitude toute information lui permettant de rectifier toute référence ou crédit dans les éditions ultérieures, de toute référence ou crédit incorrect ou omis.

Agora Books
P.O. Box 24191
300 chemin Eagleson
Kanata, Ontario K2M 2C3

Agora Books est une agence d'autoédition pour les auteurs. Elle a été fondée par Agora Cosmopolite, une société enregistrée à but non lucratif.

ISBN 978-1-927538-98-2

Imprimé au Canada

Contenu

Introduction 5

Annexe: Requête en récusation contre la juge Sylvia Corthorn . .15

Introduction

Nombreux sont les juges qui agissent de manière éthique. Cependant, Sylvia Corthorn, une juge ontarienne, ne fait de toute évidence pas partie de ceux-ci. Il n'est pas possible non plus d'affirmer que M. John Summers soit le plus juste de tous les avocats de la capitale du Canada. En effet, les activités du juge Corthorn et de M. Summers sont responsables de souffrances incalculables ayant entraîné la mort prématurée d'une femme juive noire.

Le 24 mai 2017, le juge Macleod a imploré avec une grande intégrité John Summers de vérifier de manière indépendante le bien-être et les désirs de Mme Dezrin Carby-Samuels. Cette dernière aurait été séquestrée par son mari pendant des années après qu'il l'eut rendue incapable de marcher, de parler et d'écrire tellement il avait été violent à son égard.

M. Summers a été contacté par ses « gestionnaires » qui ont organisé le remplacement du juge Macleod par la juge Corthorn. Celle-ci a saisi l'affaire dans le but d'empêcher des juges ayant une éthique professionnelle, comme le juge Macleod, de sauver la vie de Mme Carby-Samuels.

Ayant été témoin de diverses irrégularités qui suggéraient de la corruption et du racisme de la part de la juge Corthorn, le fils de Mme Carby-Samuels, qui cherchait à sauver sa mère de toute la violence conjugale infligée par M. Summers, a décidé de poursuivre la récusation de la juge Corthorn après avoir été informé des actions illicites de la juge Corthorn et de M. Summers (voir l'annexe) par un dénonciateur du palais de justice d'Ottawa.

La juge Corthorn s'est alarmée du fait que « son travail » d'escroquerie était en danger. Les preuves d'irrégularités commises par la juge Corthorn étaient si nombreuses que le juge administratif de la Cour supérieure de l'Ontario, Beaudoin, a approuvé la requête de récusation demandée par le fils de Mme Carby-Samuels.

Le fils de Mme Carby-Samuels a été contraint de poursuivre le mari de sa mère, M. Summers. En effet, après avoir déclaré avoir vu M. Summers agresser physiquement sa mère et lui infliger différentes formes de violence conjugale, M. Summers s'est arrangé pour qu'il ne puisse plus avoir de contact avec sa mère.

Pendant le procès, la juge Corthorn a fait ce que tout juge sale qui se respecte est censé faire : elle a prétendu qu'il n'existait aucune évidence qui justifiait son retrait du dossier et a autorisé John Summers à fabriquer une fausse évidence signée par Mme Georgette Cleroux, sa propre secrétaire, qui n'avait aucun statut juridique dans le dossier. La requête a ensuite été utilisée pour déclarer le fils de Mme Carby-Samuels « plaideur vexatoire » pour avoir cherché à sauver la vie de sa mère de « l'expérience médicale » que des escrocs avaient cherché à perpétuer contre Mme Carby-Samuels et son apparemment mari à « l'esprit contrôlé », qui semble avoir été programmé pour faire subir de la violence conjugale. La juge Corthorn a ensuite accéléré un « jugement sommaire » au nom de M. Summers dans le but de contrecarrer les efforts du juge Beaudoin pour la faire renvoyer de l'affaire.

En déclarant « jugement sommaire », la juge Corthorn a cherché à contrecarrer toute autre enquête judiciaire sur sa conduite quasi-criminelle, incluant des preuves de collusion avec M. Summers. La juge Corthorn a présidé un tribunal truqué dans le but de perpétuer la torture humaine. Par conséquent, l'état de Mme Carby-Samuels s'est tellement dégradé qu'elle n'était plus en mesure de marcher, de parler et d'écrire. Puis, ayant perdu toute mobilité indépendante, Mme Carby-Samuels a été forcée de souffrir et de dépérir dans une mort terrible, et ce, en étant incapable de voir son fils à la suite d'un complot criminel aux proportions démesurées.

Officiellement, M. Summers était l'avocat de M. Carby-Samuels. Toutefois, il a été reporté que M. Summers avait avoué au fils de Mme Carby-Samuels qu'il s'agissait d'une ruse et qu'il « n'était pas en mesure » de dire qui le payait.

L'esprit de M. Carby-Samuels aurait été « contrôlé », ce qui l'aurait incité à torturer sa femme. C'était apparemment la mission de M. Summers et de Mme Corthorn de contrecarrer tous les efforts des juges éthiques et du fils de Mme Carby-Samuels pour aider sa mère à aller mieux et ainsi la libérer de ce complot diabolique.

Vous pourriez penser, et avec raison, que toute cette histoire « d'esprit contrôlé » est tout simplement scandaleuse. Toutefois, des écrits portant sur des expériences de « contrôle de l'esprit

» font surface de temps en temps. Parmi ceux-ci font partie les tristement célèbres « Expériences de Montréal » de la fin des années 1950 et du début des années 1960. De toute façon, il semblerait que M. Carby-Samuels ait été la cible d'une expérience visant à retirer sa conscience de son corps, puis à la remplacer par celle d'un psychopathe. Il aurait alors commencé à battre et à torturer Mme Carby-Samuels. La preuve la plus révélatrice de cette expérience est le fait qu'une fois ce « processus de substitution » terminé, la signature de M. Carby-Samuels a radicalement changé par rapport à sa signature initiale qui avait été conservée pendant plus de 60 ans.

Le rôle de la juge Corthorn dans tout cela était par l'intermédiaire d'un « jugement sommaire ». Ce jugement a, en effet, dissimulé les témoignages écrits de plusieurs experts qui ont tous affirmé que, selon leur expertise, la signature de Horace Carby-Samuels recueillie par M. John Summers ne pouvait pas avoir été faite par la même personne que celles confirmées d'Horace Carby-Samuels faites dans le passé.

Le fils de Dezrin Carby-Samuels a commencé à soupçonner un agenda plus large lorsque Horace Carby-Samuels a commencé à exprimer sa paranoïa à propos d'une « menace extraterrestre ». Il semblerait qu'Horace Carby-Samuels ait tenté de retirer sa conscience de son corps afin de la remplacer par une autre. Cette expérience serait en réalité une opération extraterrestre manipulée.

C'est le juge Patrick Smith qui, en février 2016, a rendu un jugement par défaut en faveur du fils de Mme Carby-Samuels. Ce jugement a statué que le fils devait avoir un accès quotidien à Mme Carby-Samuels afin d'assurer le bien-être de celle-ci.

Les criminels qui cherchaient à cibler à la fois Dezrin et Horace Carby-Samuels n'aimaient pas ce jugement et voulaient Dezrin (et Horace) pour eux seuls. Ainsi, en mars 2016, ils ont utilisé John Summers pour s'assurer que la misère de Dezrin Carby-Samuels se perpétuerait par son mari dont l'esprit avait été remplacé par celui d'un psychopathe dans le but de torturer sa femme.

Le rôle de John Summers dans la mort prématurée de Dezrin Carby-Samuels est davantage documenté dans le livre *John Summers : The Untold Story of Corruption, Systemic Racism and Evil at Bell Baker LLP*.

Cela dit, la plus grande question dans tout cela est peut-être de savoir comment une mère dévouée et une infirmière retraitée qui n'a jamais eu d'agenda politique dans sa vie est devenue la cible d'un groupe criminel bien organisé, financé, aidé et encouragé par un avocat et, encore plus choquant, par un juge.

Il est évident que Mme Dezrin Carby-Samuels et son mari Horace Carby-Samuels ont été choisis par ce groupe de criminels pour une expérience médicale odieuse impliquant le contrôle de l'esprit, les abus et l'éclairage au gaz. Ces criminels ont ensuite utilisé John Summers pour concocter une défense fictive appuyée par des évidences tout aussi fictives visant à empêcher le fils du couple de les sauver du « progrès » de ces expériences. Ces expériences ont commencé sous les auspices du Dr. Jerry T.

Selon le fils de Dezrin Carby-Samuels, il était évident que sa mère était soumise à des expériences médicales bizarres. Il l'a réalisé après avoir lu des critiques à propos de ce médecin qui a la réputation d'expérimenter sur des cobayes. D'ailleurs, ces critiques ont suscité la colère de ses anciens patients qui ont réussi à s'échapper. Ces derniers ont remarqué que leur état s'était grandement amélioré après avoir cessé de voir le Dr. J.

C'est alors que le fils de Dezrin Carby-Samuels a réalisé que s'il pouvait libérer sa mère du contrôle de ce médecin, elle pourrait profiter d'un rétablissement aussi rapide que celui dont avaient bénéficié les autres cobayes.

Grâce à ces expériences, Mme Carby-Samuels est passée d'une femme en très bonne santé qui s'attendait à vivre aussi longtemps que sa grand-mère qui a vécu 104 ans, à une femme complètement estropiée et détruite, laissée à pourrir dans ses propres matières fécales. Aujourd'hui, elle se trouve dans un cimetière juif d'Ottawa, au Canada.

Il n'est pas possible de connaitre l'identité de la personne qui versait les 300$/heure que John Summers avait donné au fils de Mme Carby-Samuels, mais leurs plans sont évidents.

L'Allemagne nazie n'avait pas seulement cherché à exterminer le peuple juif et d'autres minorités. Cet empire maléfique avait également cherché à mener d'horribles expériences médicales parallèlement à un programme d'extermination.

Lorsque l'Allemagne nazie s'est soi-disant rendue aux alliés, il est bien connu que les mêmes scientifiques qui ont mené des expériences grotesques sur des vies humaines ont été recrutés par des criminels qui ont cherché à poursuivre ces expériences sur des groupes ciblés sans méfiance, y compris des populations vulnérables comme les personnes âgées, les sans-abris et les communautés minoritaires impuissantes.

Les « Expériences de Montréal » sont peut-être l'exemple le plus officiel et le plus public de la poursuite des expériences nazies.

L'exécution du complot impliquant un avocat d'Ottawa et une juge de la Cour supérieure de l'Ontario rappelle la série *Blacklist,* de Jon Bokenkamp. Dans cette série, on y présente un monde dirigé par des criminels qui dirigent des gouvernements et de grandes entreprises à travers une clique de surveillance.

De tels criminels financent et préparent certaines personnes à des postes prestigieux et lorsqu'ils finissent par obtenir les postes souhaités, ces « archontes » commencent alors à exiger des faveurs qui peuvent parfois inclure l'utilisation d'individus vulnérables et de communautés minoritaires pour des expériences médicales. Ces expériences sont à l'abri de tout contrôle juridique par les agents stratégiquement recrutés.

Blacklist était apparemment si proche de la vérité que même si la série a été filmée en 2013, elle inclue un épisode dans lequel un virus est libéré d'un laboratoire en Chine. Cela déclenche une pandémie et un informateur scientifique chinois cherche refuge aux États-Unis, alléguant que le complot pandémique est le résultat du génie génétique. Dans la version de *Blacklist*, les Américains ont utilisé les informations de l'informateur chinois qu'ils ont aidé à s'échapper de la Chine pour arrêter complètement la pandémie.

En 2020, Dr. Li-Meng Yan, un informateur, a fait la même allégation que celle dans *Blacklist.* Étrangement, il a un nom qui ressemble au scientifique chinois de *Blacklist.* Or, cette fois-ci, la population n'a pas réagi de la même manière que dans la série populaire.

Un vieux proverbe dit : « Ceux qui ignorent les leçons de l'histoire sont condamnés à la répéter. »

Dr. Michael Salla a également remarqué un jour que « la science-fiction cache la vérité à la vue de tous ».

Afin de sauver notre monde des cerveaux criminels qui sont responsables des expériences invasives contre les humains, il est vital que nous, en tant qu'humains, commencions à tirer des leçons de l'histoire et à rechercher la vérité qui se cache de nous.

Dezrin Carby-Samuels est devenu la dernière victime noire et juive d'un crime contre l'humanité. Ce crime a été commis par ceux qui cherchent à renverser l'état de droit par la manipulation de juges, d'avocats, de policiers, de chefs religieux, de dirigeants d'entreprise et de politiciens.

Les Païens gnostiques ont appelé le groupe qui aurait pris contrôle de l'esprit d'au moins un avocat et un juge de la Cour supérieure de l'Ontario les Archontes, ou, plus précisément, le « visage humanisé des extraterrestres manipulateurs » tel que présenté dans les recherches approfondies de John Lash sur Metahistory.org.

Corthorn et John Summers ont été insérés dans la vie d'une famille juive noire au nom d'une « cinquième colonne » démoniaque. Tant que l'argent coulait à flots et que leur sécurité d'emploi était assurée, ils ne se souciaient pas de la souffrance humaine ni de la torture engendrée par leurs activités infâmes.

« Black Lives Matter » est devenu un slogan qui a émergé des meurtres de personnes noires innocentes aux mains d'agents qui sont des membres des forces de police. Il est évident que la vie des noirs n'avait pas d'importance aux yeux de Corthorn J. et de John Summers ainsi qu'à ceux des autres agents nommés dans le livre *John Summers: The Untold Story of Corruption, Systemic Racism and Evil at Bell Baker LLP*, qui sont tous liés entre eux.

Le fait qu'un juge et qu'un avocat de l'Ontario aient utilisé leur pouvoir conféré par Sa Majesté la Reine du Canada pour se rendre complices d'un complot diabolique qui a été reconnu par le juge administratif Beaudoin comme légitime représente une trahison choquante de leurs serments d'office.

Ce livre contient la preuve qui a été approuvée par le juge Beaudoin. Toutefois, la juge Corthorn nie l'existence de ces preuves (voir l'annexe).

Avec tout le respect qu'il leur doit, l'auteur de ce livre croit que Madame la juge Corthorn ne devrait pas présider une salle d'audience qui prétend être légale et que M. Summers ne devrait pas exercer le droit dans la province de l'Ontario. Selon lui, le rôle de Corthorn J et de M. Summers dans la mort prématurée de la femme juive noire à la suite d'activités néfastes nécessite soit leur démission, soit leur révocation par les procureurs de la Couronne, et ce, en accord avec l'intégrité de la base constitutionnelle de lois canadiennes.

Annexe

Requête en récusation contre la juge Sylvia Corthorn

Search results	Archive	Collapse	Delete	Spam	Johanson, Tina (JUD)
					TinaJohanson@ontario...
					Search emails

OFFICIAL LEGAL NOTICE / DEMAND LETTER - ... (5)

cosmopolita cosmopolita Dear Ontario Supe	Oct 5 at 10:10 AM	
cosmopolita cosmopolita Corrected letter - r	Oct 5 at 10:17 AM	+ 3 more contacts
Johanson, Tina (JUD) <Tina.Johanson@ontario.ca>	Oct 5 at 12:34 PM	

To cosmopolita cosmopolita, Creswell, Leslie (JUD)
CC John Summers, Gorette Cleroux

Good afternoon,

I have your email message of October 5, 2017. The method by which to request that a judge consider recusing himself or herself from a matter is not by way of email or letter communication. To obtain an order from a judge recusing himself or herself, you are required to bring a motion. The motion must be before the judge whom you are asking to recuse themselves -- in this case, Justice Corthorn. The motion must be supported by an evidentiary record.

Therefore, if it is your intention to request Justice Corthorn to recuse herself, you are required to serve and file the appropriate motion record. Service is required on all parties to the matter or matters for which you are requesting that Justice Corthorn recuse herself.

Please note that further correspondence to me or Ms. Creswell on this issue would be inappropriate. You are required to deal with the civil counter on the matter.

Sincerely,

Tina Johanson

SCJ Trial Coordinator / Coordonnatrice des procès de la CSJ
Criminal and Civil Divisions / affaires criminelles et civiles
Tina.Johanson@ontario.ca

> Show original message

← Reply ← Reply to All → Forward ••• More

cosmopolita cosmopolita Dear Tina, Thanks	Oct 5 at 1:06 PM	
Johanson, Tina (JUD) Mr. Carby-Samuels, The	Oct 5 at 2:12 PM	

Click to Reply, Reply All or Forward

FILE NUMBER: 15-667

ONTARIO

SUPERIOR COURT OF JUSTICE

BETWEEN

RAYMOND CARBY-SAMUELS

Plaintiff

- and –

HORACE R CARBY-SAMUELS

Defendant

AFFIDAVIT OF RAYMOND CARBY-SAMUELS

I, of the City of Ottawa in the Province of Ontario, MAKE OATH AND SAY (or AFFIRM):

1. I, **Raymond Carby-Samuels**, confirm and attest to the fact that I have a reasonable apprehension of bias regarding the expressed ability of Justice Sylvia Corthorn to preside over the fair and impartial administration of justice as outlined by the Canadian Judicial Council's Code of Ethics.
2. I submit this Motion seeking the immediate and if possible retroactive recusal of Justice Sylvia Corthorn on all matters related to the Defence Counsel's Motions for Summary Judgement and Vexatious Litigant, and ar

other matter related to Court File 15-66772 based upon the legal advisement of Tina Johanson, SCJ Trial Coordinator, Criminal and Civil Divisions of the Superior Court of Justice in Ottawa. [Exhibit 1]

3. I made a complaint to the Canadian Judicial Council dated 6 October 2017 outlining grounds for Justice Sylvia Corthorn's immediate recusal from Court File 15-66772. [Exhibit 2]

4. DISCRIMINATION - Justice Corthorn subjected me to *prima facie* discrimination involving differential treatment as defined by the *Ontario Human Rights Code* by fabricating a "Leave for Urgent Motion" process that is not authorized by the *Ontario Rules of Civil Procedure*; has no apparent legal precedent in common law and gave the appearance of handicapping my efforts pursue my Motion as a self-represented litigant.

5. INSTITUTIONALIZED RACISM / DISCRIMNATION – Whereas Justice Macloed on 24 March 2017 sought to endorse his sought independent verification of my Mom's well-being to ensure that my Mom has not been held "prisoner" to borrow his words, Justice Corthorn expressed no such interest in verifying the safety and security of my Mom, as a black woman, pursuant to the *Canadian Charter of Rights and Freedoms* and have the appearance of racism. Justice Corthorn apparent lack of demonstrated concern for the factual verification of my Mom's well-being and desires that is incumbent of any Judge that seeks to uphold our Constitution requires her immediate recusal. Furthermore, Justice Corthorn gave no regard to the physical disabilities of my Mom in being able to present herself in the Courtroom in violation of Equality Rights stipulated in Section 15(1) of the *Canadian Charter of Rights and Freedoms* while ignoring my presented written evidence of my Mom's desires in lieu of her attendance.

6. APPARENT PREJUDICE IN FAVOUR OF DEFENCE. Justice Sylvia Corthorn on multiple occasions demonstrated apparent bias. This included allowing the Defence to submit documents late in respect of the *Ontario Rules of Civil Procedure* which is based upon supporting a fair litigation process. While Justice Corthorn allowed Defence Counsel to submit late documents, in Justice Corthorn's ruling on the Leave for Urgent Motion, she scolded the Plaintiff who is a self-represented litigant for having made a late submission as a result of the tardiness of the Plaintiff's lawyer who he had no control over. Justice Corthorn also accepted the veracity of claims made by

Defence Counsel regarding the wishes of the Plaintiff's Mom as being the same as the Defendant when she referred to "my parents" in No 11 of her so-called Leave for Urgent Motion ruling even though the Defence Counsel had refused to independently verify the well-being and desires of my Mom. Justice Corthorn therefore has demonstrated a penchant to rule in favour of Defence Counsel without any basis of facts / evidence while disregarding my evidence regarding the stated desires of my Mom.

7. ACCEPTANCE OF APPARENT FAKE SIGNATURE – I have observed by meticulous consistence of my father's signature over the years. Justice Corthorn accepted an affidavit during the Leave for Urgent Motion which was not only late; and contained false information but also contained a signature which in no way resembled signatures by the Defendant that have been consistent in previous Affidavits of the Defendant.

8. KNOWINGLY ACCEPTING FRAUDULENT REPRESENTATION IN AN AFFIDAVIT – Justice Corthon has accepted affidavits knowingly with false information proving a willingness to use this false information to support an Endorsement that has been subjected to prejudice. Examples of Justice Corthorn knowingly accepting Defence Counsel's false information to prejudice the Plaintiff include the Defence Affidavits references to "my parents" not wanting to see or have contact with me when she knew that the Defendant rejected Judge Macloed's sought independent verification; and the Defendant's Affidavit fraudulently alleging that I had been "blacklisted" by Ottawa Ambulance Services even though I presented official correspondence from Ottawa Ambulance Services denying such a "blacklisting". Furthermore, even though Defence Counsel has claimed that the Defendant wants to have no contact with the Plaintiff, Justice Corthorn ignored evidence presented by the Plaintiff that the Defendant actually called the Plaintiff on 21 August 2017 and talked for over two minutes. This is clear proof that Defence Counsel's representation concerning the alleged desire of the Defendant not to have contact as being fraudulent. [Exhibit 2]

9. THE ACCEPTANCE OF INADMISSIBLE AFFIDAVITS submitted by Defence Counsel in support of their Motions for Summary Judgement and Vexatious Litigation. Justice Corthorn has shown a lack of respect for me as a self-represented litigant pursuant to Section 24 of the *Canadian Charter of Rights and Freedoms* by allowing Defence Council to run amok of

established practices of proper Affidavits in relation to the *Ontario Rules of Civil Procedure*. This includes Justice Corthorn allowing Defence Counsel to submit an affidavit by Gorette Cleroux who works for John Summers whose testimony is based upon heresay she skimmed online. At the same time, Justice Corthorn has allowed Defence Council to unilaterally block my own *bona fide* affidavit submissions.

10. DENIAL OF MY RIGHT TO LEGAL REPRESENTATION – My lawyer had sought to seek an adjournment of the Motions for Summary Judgement of Vexatious Litigation to allow him time to prepare since he had take so much time to prepare the Urgent Motion. Justice Corthorn denied my lawyer's request and then forced me to defend myself against Motions for Summary Judgement and Vexatious Litigation against a lawyer who apparently was accepted to the Bar in 1999.

Affirmed before me at the City of Ottawa in the Province of Ontario on _____OCT 1 0 2017_____

_____
Commissioner for Taking Affidavits

_____
(Signature of deponent)

							Johanson, Tina (JUD)
← Search results	←	≪	→	🗄 Archive	⊞ Collapse 🗑 Delete	🚫 Sp	✉ TinaJohanson@ontario...
●	OFFICIAL LEGAL NOTICE / DEMAND LETTER - ... (5)					★	🔍 Search emails
↳	cosmopolita cosmopolita	Dear Ontario Supe			Oct 5 at 10:10 AM	★	•••
↳	cosmopolita cosmopolita	Corrected letter - r			Oct 5 at 10:17 AM	★	+ 3 more contacts
↳	Johanson, Tina (JUD) <TinaJohanson@ontario.ca>				Oct 5 at 12:34 PM	★	

To cosmopolita cosmopolita, Creswell, Leslie (JUD)
CC John Summers, Gorette Cleroux

Good afternoon,

I have your email message of October 5, 2017. The method by which to request that a judge consider recusing himself or herself from a matter is not by way of email or letter communication. To obtain an order from a judge recusing himself or herself, you are required to bring a motion. The motion must be before the judge whom you are asking to recuse themselves – in this case, Justice Corthorn. The motion must be supported by an evidentiary record.

Therefore, if it is your intention to request Justice Corthorn to recuse herself, you are required to serve and file the appropriate motion record. Service is required on all parties to the matter or matters for which you are requesting that Justice Corthorn recuse herself.

Please note that further correspondence to me or Ms. Creswell on this issue would be inappropriate. You are required to deal with the civil counter on the matter.

Sincerely,

Tina Johanson

SCJ Trial Coordinator / Coordonnatrice des procès de la CSJ
Criminal and Civil Divisions / affaires criminelles et civiles
TinaJohanson@ontario.ca

› Show original message

← Reply   ≪ Reply to All   → Forward   ••• More

●	cosmopolita cosmopolita Dear Tina, Thanks	Oct 5 at 1:06 PM	⋮
●	Johanson, Tina (JUD) Mr. Carby-Samuels, Th	Oct 5 at 2:12 PM	⋮

Court File: 15-66772

B.P 24191 – 300 Eagleson Rd
Kanata, Ontario K2M 2C3

6 October 2017

Canadian Judicial Council,
Ottawa, Ontario, K1A 0W8

Complaint Against Justice Sylvia Corthorn

Dear Canadian Judicial Council representative,

I very respectfully submit a complaint to your Office regarding apparent judicial misconduct and breaches in violation of the *Canadian Judicial Council's Code of Ethics*.

I'm requesting a full investigation of Justice Corthon's treatment of my Court Claim since Her Honour had seized my Claim without my voluntary consent.

I'm hoping that Justice Sylvia Corthorn will voluntarily recuse herself from presiding any further on my Court File 15-66772 on the Ontario Superior Court of Justice in matters specifically relating to my sought Urgent Motion to visit my elderly and sick mother and in general matters related prevailing Defence Motions.

Justice Sylvia Corthorn has totally disregarded the prior endorsement of Justice Macloed who sought independent verification to borrow His Honour's words that my Mother "is not being held prisoner" by my father. [Exhibit 1 – attached]

In doing so, Justice Corthorn to-date has acted in callous disregard of my Mom's life, and in general, the rights of the physically disabled and the plight of women suffering from spousal abuse and human decency along with my own civil rights.

Justice Corthorn for months has perpetuated the abuse of my Mom that she has been subjected to by my father in addition to the subversion of my own rights.

Evidence that I submitted to Justice Corthorn regarding abuse and neglect involving enforced social isolation and deprivation of access to medical care by the Defendant that my Mom had sought to protect her health have been of no apparent concern to this Judge. This blocking of access to medical care has involved the
depriving of speech therapy which resulted in my Mom losing the ability to talk.

Justice Corthorn has denied my Mom her civil rights prescribed in Section 7 regarding "Life, liberty and the security of person" by showing total disregard to my Mom's complaints of abuse and my efforts to establish contact with my Mom, which Her Honour has no basis in law to frustrate, in violation of my freedom of conscience and religion as affirmed in the *Canadian Charter of Rights and Freedoms*.

In Justice Corthon's decision [no 11], she referred to what "my parents" want in relationship to my Mother when she has no basis of fact to be making this reference.

The Defendant denied Justice's MacLoed stated endorsement in the transcript attached of my 24 March 2017 Motion to support a process of independent verification to ensure to borrow His Honour's words that my Mom is "not being held prisoner".

It is therefore a categorical demonstration of prejudice and bias for Justice Corthorn to then make a claim of what "my parents" [i.e. cited in no 11 of her Ruling -- Exhibit 2] want solely based on the veracity of Defendant's heresay claims in his affidavit that he has sought to block independent verification.

Justice Corthon has shown in Her Honour's ruling that unlike Justice Macloed, she will not be guided by evidence and facts. Instead, Justice Corthorn has shown a prejudicial bias in support of / in favour of any and all claims of the Defendant irrespective of any evidence to the contrary.

I have presented evidence to Justice Corthorn that my Mom has maintained a desire to see me. But instead, Justice Corthorn has made misleading statements regarding the desires of my Mom without any basis of fact or evidence.

There is no greater responsibility entrusted to Judges across Canada under our *Canadian Charter of Rights and Freedoms* that the protection of life.

The Supreme Court of Canada has affirmed that judges are required to use their inherent jurisdiction to affirm the protection of life and especially in matters regarding children and the physically disabled like my Mom; and Justice Corthorn has failed miserably in her Oath to Her Majesty which is implicitly based on this axiom.

Furthermore, Justice Corthorn elected to base her decision on an Affidavit submitted by Defence Counsel that was late in violation of the *Ontario Rules of Civil Procedure*, contained verifiable slander alleging that I had been "blacklisted" by the Ottawa Ambulance Services" [Exhibit 4] and according to my Handwriting experts, the signed Affidavit was subject to forgery. [Exhibit 3].

In her ruling, Justice Corthorn sought to chastise the lateness of my lawyer who had been preparing the Urgent Motion but failed to similar chastise the repeated lateness of Defence Counsel in violation of Civil Procedure which further shows bias.

I would also add that Justice Corthorn has subjected me to differential treatment in violation of the Ontario Human Rights Code by requiring that my Urgent Motion be submitted first through a "Leave of Urgent Motion" to Her Honour. There's no such thing in the Ontario Rules of Civil Procedure as a "Leave of Urgent Motion" which she contrived in violation of my civil rights and supports a reasonable apprehension of bias

I hope that Justice Corthorn will do the Honorable thing and immediately recuse hersel from having subjected me to bias and prejudice in her Courtroom and for having perpetuated the abuse of my Mother which had resulted in my reasonable apprehensic of bias against her ability to treat my file based upon actual evidence and facts, and to affirm my desire for equity pursuant to Section 96 of the Courts of Justice Act

Thanks for your consideration.

Kind regards,

Raymond Carby-Samuels

cc. Office of Justice Corthorn

Offices of MacNamara, JS

EXPERT AFFIDAVIT OF GRACIE CARR

STATE OF NEW YORK

COUNTY OF BROOME

BE IT KNOWN, that on this 10th day of September 2017.

BEFORE ME, a duly sworn and competent authority in and for the County of Broome, NOTARY PUBLIC, and the undersigned affiant and competent witness appearing herein below,

DID PERSONALLY APPEAR: GRACE CARR, a person of fully age of Majority, residing and domiciled in the State of New York, County of Broome.

WHO AFTER BEEN DULY SWORN BY ME, did depose and state:

(1) My name is Dr Grace Carr and I have personal knowledge of the matters contained in this Affidavit. I am a licensed and practicing Forensic Expert in detecting forged signature in the State of New York. I have been practicing as a Forensic Expert for 10 years. I am over the age of eighteen years, am of sound mind, having never been convicted of a felony or a crime of moral turpitude; I am competent in all respect to make this declaration. I have personal knowledge of the matters herein.

(2) I have studied, trained and hold a certification in the examination, comparison, analysis and identification of Signatures from The International School of Forensic Document Examination. I have served as an expert within pending litigation matters.

(3) I was asked to compare the signature on Exhibit A, Exhibit B and Exhibit C. After carefully examining and analyzing the signature in Exhibit A, Exhibit B and Exhibit C. It is my opinion that the signatures of Mr. Horace Carby-Samuels in three different documentation are resulted from three different timelines.

(4) In the first documentation is Court File no. 1771624 which seems to hold the original signature of Mr. Horace Carby-Samuels (exhibit A) Similarly in the second documentation, Court File no.15-66772 (exhibit B) which has the alleged false signature along with the third documentation with the same Court File no. 15-66772(exhibit C) which has been used as preference for additional clarity.

(5) From the basic analysis, the first and third documents are signed by the same individual however; it seems to be clear that the second documentation has a forged signature. According to the formal analysis this type of forgery of signature would be classified as the simulated signature, or "free hand forgery" as it is sometime known. This forgery is constructed by using a genuine signature as a model. The forger generates an artistic reproduction of this model. Depending on his skill and amount of practice, the simulation may be quite good and bear remarkable pictorial similarity to the genuine signature.

(6) Many simulations created with a model at hand will contain at least some of the general indicators of forgery, such as tremor, hesitation, pen lifts, blunt starts and stops, patching, and static pressure. They will have a slow "drawn" appearance. The practiced simulation is most often a higher quality creation in that the model signature has been memorized and some of the movements used to produce it have become semi-automatic. This simulation can be written with a more natural fluid manner. There can be tapered starts and stops, changes in pen pressure, and much less tremor in the moving line. Speed lends fluidity to writing. The more rapidly the pen moves while creating the genuine writing or signature, the more difficult the genuine writing is to imitate. Rapidly formed movements are scrutinized more closely than slower counterparts. A slowly written signature is not only easier for the forger to duplicate with some fashionable degree of pictorial similarity; the product will also display indications of non-genuineness than the forgery of a rapid and fluidly executed signature. The writer of a simulation must, of necessity, pay more attention to the form of a letter than the speed of his pen.

(7) Both practiced and non-practiced simulations will still have notable shortcomings. The forger naturally puts his greatest effort into those parts of the name that he expects to fall under the greatest scrutiny. Although letter forms (especially the more prominent, large or beginning letters) may almost duplicate the genuine letters, proportions and height ratios will seldom be correct. Internal portions of the names (smaller, less prominent letters and pen movements) will usually display the greatest divergence from the correct form and movements found in the genuine signature. During the creation of a simulated forgery, the author attempts to duplicate the writing style of another individual. By doing this, the forger leaves behind little, if any, of his own distinctive writing style. By doing an emulation of someone else's signature, he also produces one of the best of all possible disguises of his own handwriting. Infrequently, some of the forger's own individual characteristics may appear in the disputed writing. The limited quantity of these characteristics which appear on those occasions is such that identification of the author almost never occurs. If there are a sufficient number of significant differences between the questioned signature and the genuine signatures, and these same differences appear in the practiced simulations, there may be a basis to associate the forgery to the forger within some degree of probability. An absolute identification, nonetheless, even under these circumstances is infrequent.

(8) Closely related to this form of identification process is that of determining the number of different forgers from a quantity of simulations. On occasion there will be two or more forgers attempting to reproduce the same signature. It may be possible to group or associate simulations of the same name by the combinations of defects within the forgeries. By associating and grouping the similar defects (when compared to the genuine signature) it may be possible to conclude and illustrate that there are indeed, two or more different forgers.

(9) The second documentation (Exhibit 2) clearly projects the forged signature for the following reasoning

In the second document it can identified that the forger places the pen point in contact with the paper, and then starts writing. When he or she is finished with the name or some portion thereof, he or she stops the pen and lifts it from the surface. This has cause the emphasized blunt start and ending where the pen was placed in contact with the surface. At times this contact is held so long that the pen contains two fluid inks in the front letter of the signature, it has wet the paper and migrate outward from the contact point.

There may be unnecessary and extraneous marks caused by pen starts and stops. The writer may decided after putting his or her pen in contact with the paper, that it is in the wrong spot, picks it up and moves it to a position considered more correct. Normally a signature's starts and stops are much more dynamic which can be noticed in the other two documents. The pen is moving horizontally before it contacts the paper and is lifted at the end while still in flight. This leaves a tapered appearance at the beginnings and endings of names or letters.

In this situation it can occasioned that the pen stops at an unusual point in the writing; perhaps during radical change in direction is about to take a new letter formation is about to be started. This may take on the appearance of a larger gap in the written line where one is not expected, or an overlapping of two ink lines where there should be only one continuous line which clearly in the second document but not the other two, where it seems to be following the same pattern throughout the signature.

Because the creation of most forms of non-genuine signatures are little more than drawings, the pen is moving so slowly that small, sometimes microscopic changes in direction take place in what should be a fluid-looking line. The resultant line is not smooth, but reflects the "shaking" pen. It can be seen that the lines in the signature of the second documentation is much larger than the rest two and has microscopic shakes.

Again, because the pen is moving slowly rather than with the dynamic movement associated with most genuine writings, the ink line remains constant in thickness, resulting from the same constant pressure exerted on a slowly moving pen. There will be little, if any, tapering of internal lines. This is clearly evident in the second document's signature which constantly remains in the same thickness.

Sometimes when the genuine writer makes an error while writing our own signature, more commonly individuals may leave the signature alone, caring little about the mistake or imperfection, while others will simply "fix" the signature by correcting the offending portion. This might have been done in this situation to make the signature more readable, or because a defect in the pen or paper has affected what we perceive to be our "normal" signature, or for some other reason that may even be subconscious.

However by analyzing the previous signature that seems very unlikely. These "fixes" are patent, with no attempt made on the part of the writer to mask or otherwise hide the correction for which some letters are crossing the others out.

These signature corrections are quite different than the patching that is frequently found in non-genuine signatures. On these occasions, the writer is not attempting to make the signature more readable, but to make its appearance passable. He or she is fixing an obvious defect that he or she perceives as detectable, and might uncover his fraudulent product and foil his scheme. These usually take the form of a correction to a flaw in the writing line rather than in the form of a letter. Extensions to entry or terminal strokes, or to lower descending portions of letters, along with corrections to embellishments, are typical of non-genuine patching.

It is my professional opinion that the documentation in (exhibit B) has a forged signature of Mr. Horace R. Carby-Samuels and with intent of malicious actions.

Dated: September 10, 2017

I affirm the truth of this statement

GRACE CARR

STATE OF NEW YORK

COUNTY OF BROOME

I, the undersigned Notary Public, in and for the said State and County, hereby certify that Dr Grace Carr whose name is signed to the foregoing Affidavit, and who is known to me, acknowledged before me on this day that, being informed of said Affidavit, He executed same voluntarily on the day the same bears date.

Given under my hand and seal this 10th day of September, 2017

Kieran Ryan

Notary Public

To: The Ontario Supreme Court of Justice

From:

Date: September 16th 2017

Re: Horace R. Carby-Samuels v. Raymond Carby-Samuels, Court file no. 17-71624, Court file no. 1566772

ISSUE

Mr. Raymond Carby Samuels has brought forward the following documents in Exhibit A, Exhibit B and Exhibit C for investigation in the claims of forgery of the signatures of Mr. Horace R. Carby-Samuels.

From handwriting experts reports it has been analysed the signature of Mr. Horace Carby-Samuels in three different documentation are resulted from three different timelines.

In the first documentation is Court File no. 1771624 which seems to hold the original signature of Mr Horace Carby-Samuels (exhibit A)

Similarly in the second documentation, Court File no.15-66772 (exhibit B) which has the alleged false signature along with the third documentation with the same Court File no. 15-66772(exhibit C) which has been used as preference for additional clarity.

From the basic analysis, the first and third documents are signed by the same individual however; it seems to be clear that the second documentation has a forged signature.

BRIEF ANSWER

According to the formal analysis this type of forgery of signature would be classified as the simulated signature, or "free hand forgery" as it is sometime known. This forgery is constructed by using a genuine signature as a model. The forger generates an artistic reproduction of this model. Depending on his skill and amount of practice, the simulation may be quite good and bear remarkable pictorial similarity to the genuine signature.

Many simulations created with a model at hand will contain at least some of the general indicators of forgery, such as tremor, hesitation, pen lifts, blunt starts and stops, patching, and static pressure. They will have a slow "drawn" appearance. The practiced simulation is most often a higher quality creation in that the model signature has been memorized and some of the movements used to produce it have become semi-automatic. This simulation can be written with a more natural fluid manner. There can be tapered starts and stops, changes in pen pressure, and much less tremor in the moving line. Speed lends fluidity to writing. The more rapidly the pen moves while creating the genuine writing or signature, the more difficult the genuine writing is to imitate. Rapidly formed movements are scrutinized more closely than slower counterparts. A slowly written signature is not only easier for the forger to duplicate with some fashionable degree of pictorial similarity; the product will also display indications of non-genuineness than the forgery of a rapid and fluidly executed signature. The writer of a simulation must, of necessity, pay more attention to the form of a letter than the speed of his pen.

Both practiced and non-practiced simulations will still have notable shortcomings. The forger naturally puts his greatest effort into those parts of the name that he expects to fall under the greatest scrutiny. Although letter forms (especially the more prominent, large or beginning letters) may almost duplicate the genuine letters, proportions and height ratios will seldom be correct. Internal portions of the names (smaller, less prominent letters and pen movements) will usually display the greatest divergence from the correct form and movements found in the genuine signature.

During the creation of a simulated forgery, the author attempts to duplicate the writing style of another individual. By doing this, the forger leaves behind little, if any, of his own distinctive writing style. By doing an emulation of someone else's signature, he also produces one of the best of all possible disguises of his own handwriting. Infrequently, some of the forger's own individual characteristics may appear in the disputed writing. The limited quantity of these characteristics which appear on those occasions is such that identification of the author almost never occurs.

If there are a sufficient number of significant differences between the questioned signature and the genuine signatures, and these same differences appear in the practiced simulations, there may be a basis to associate the forgery to the forger within some degree of probability. An absolute identification, nonetheless, even under these circumstances is infrequent.

Closely related to this form of identification process is that of determining the number of different forgers from a quantity of simulations. On occasion there will be two or more forgers attempting to reproduce the same signature. It may be possible to group or associate simulations of the same name by the combinations of defects within the forgeries. By associating and grouping the similar defects (when compared to the genuine signature) it may be possible to conclude and illustrate that there are indeed, two or more different forgers.

REASONING OF FACTS

The second documentation (exhibit 2) clearly projects the forged signature for the following reasoning

1. **Blunt starts and stops**

    In the second document it can identified that the forger places the pen point in contact with the paper, and then starts writing. When he is finished with the name or some portion thereof, he stops the pen and lifts it from the surface. This has cause the emphasized blunt start and ending where the pen was placed in contact with the surface. At times this contact is held so long that the pen contains two fluid ink in the front letter of the signature, it has wet the paper and migrate outward from the contact point.

There may be unnecessary and extraneous marks caused by pen starts and stops. The writer may decided after putting his pen in contact with the paper, that it is in the wrong spot, picks it up and moves it to a position considered more correct. Normally a signature's starts and stops are much more dynamic which can be noticed in the other two documents. The pen is moving horizontally before it contacts the paper and is lifted at the end while still in flight. This leaves a tapered appearance at the beginnings and endings of names or letters.

2. **Pen lifts and hesitation**

In this situation it can occasioned that the pen stops at an unusual point in the writing; perhaps during radical change in direction is about to take a new letter formation is about to be started. This may take on the appearance of a larger gap in the written line where one is not expected, or an overlapping of two ink lines where there should be only one continuous line which clearly in the second document but not the other two, where it seems to be following the same pattern throughout the signature .

3. **Tremor- minor shaking**

Because the creation of most forms of non-genuine signatures are little more than drawings, the pen is moving so slowly that small, sometimes microscopic changes in direction take place in what should be a fluid-looking line. The resultant line is not smooth, but reflects the "shaking" pen. It can be seen that the lines in the signature of the second documentation is much larger than the rest two and has microscopic shakes.

4. **Speed and pressure**

Again, because the pen is moving slowly rather than with the dynamic movement associated with most genuine writings, the ink line remains constant in thickness, resulting from the same constant pressure exerted on a slowly moving pen. There will be little, if any, tapering of internal lines. This is clearly evident in the second document's signature which constantly remains in the same thickness.

5. **Patching**

Sometimes when the genuine writer makes an error while writing our own signature, more commonly individuals may leave the signature alone, caring little about the mistake or imperfection, while others will simply "fix" the signature by correcting the offending portion. This might have be done this situation to make the signature more readable, or because a defect in the pen or paper has affected what we perceive to be our "normal" signature, or for some other reason that may even be subconscious.

However by analysing the previous signature that seems very unlikely. These "fixes" are patent, with no attempt made on the part of the writer to mask or otherwise hide the correction for which some letters are crossing the others out.

These signature corrections are quite different than the patching that is frequently found in non-genuine signatures. On these occasions, the writer is not attempting to make the signature more readable, but to make its appearance passable. He is fixing an obvious defect that he perceives as detectable, and might uncover his fraudulent product and foil his scheme. These usually take the form of a correction to a flaw in the writing line rather than in the form of a letter. Extensions to entry or terminal strokes, or to lower descending portions of letters, along with corrections to embellishments, are typical of non-genuine patching.

DISCUSSION

Penalty for Counterfeiting and Forgery in Canada

Each and every case of fraud is different and may result in varied consequences, however in this current scenario it is extremely vivid that the documentation was created for malicious reasoning. Therefore an individual can expect extensive prison time, as well as fines and community service work, or restitution. Other social consequences follow such as a criminal record limiting the ability to travel, and the difficulty in finding employment.

The Criminal Code of Canada states:

368(1) Uttering forged document

368(1) Every one who, knowing that a document is forged,

(a) uses, deals with or acts on it, or

(b) causes or attempts to cause any person to use, deal with or act on it, as if the document were genuine, is guilty of an indictable offence and liable to imprisonment for a term not exceeding fourteen years.

368(2) Wherever forged

368(2) For the purposes of proceedings under this section, the place where a document was forged is not material.

R.S., 1985, c. C-46, s. 368; 1992, c. 1, s. 60(F).

369 Exchequer bill paper, public seals, etc.

369 Every one who, without lawful authority or excuse, the proof of which lies on him,

(a) makes, uses or knowingly has in his possession

(i) any exchequer bill paper, revenue paper or paper that is used to make bank-notes, or

(ii) any paper that is intended to resemble paper mentioned in subparagraph (i),

(b) makes, offers or disposes of or knowingly has in his possession any plate, die, machinery, instrument or other writing or material that is adapted and intended to be used to commit forgery, or

(c) makes, reproduces or uses a public seal of Canada or of a province, or the seal of a public body or authority in Canada, or of a court of law, is guilty of an indictable offence and liable to imprisonment for a term not exceeding fourteen years. R.S., c. C-34, s. 327.

370 Counterfeit proclamation, etc.

370 Every one who knowingly

(a) prints any proclamation, order, regulation or appointment, or notice thereof, and causes it falsely to purport to have been printed by the Queen's Printer for Canada or the Queen's Printer for a province, or

(b) tenders in evidence a copy of any proclamation, order, regulation or appointment that falsely purports to have been printed by the Queen's Printer for Canada or the Queen's Printer for a province, is guilty of an indictable offence and liable to imprisonment for a term not exceeding five years. R.S., c. C-34, s. 328.

Interpretation of the Offence

Actus Reus

The act of forging the signature would be applicable enough to be considered as Actus reus for committing the act of forgery. (R v JJV, 1994 CanLII 6514 (NB CA))

Mens Rea

The mens res for forgery under s. 366(1) requires an "intent to deceive" which requires an intent that is more than mere "carelessness or negligence". The intent to deceive should generally "be coupled with an intent that the document be used to someone's prejudice, or that a person be induced to act in a certain way." Prejudice need not result as long as there was an intent for the document to be treated as genuine.(R v Benson (M.) et al., 2012 MBCA 94 (CanLII))

The Crown must show the "falsity of the endorsement the document has been shown to be a forged document and its use with knowledge is sufficient to show the commission of the offence." (R v Elkin (1978), 42 C.C.C. (2d) 185 (B.C.C.A.))

The accused must have known that "the document was false and intended for somebody to act upon it as if it was genuine.".(Sebo, [1988] A.J. No. 475 (C.A.))

It is not necessary that the accused "intended" to defraud anyone. (R v Atwal, [2015] O.J. No. 3748 (C.J.) R v G.T., 2016 CanLII 82183 (NL PC) at para 59 per Gorman PCJ)

From the situation it can be concluded that the documentation were falsely created with intent to harm the applicant

"False documents"

A fake or false item that was made as a "novelty" item cannot be a "false document" and the creation of which does not carry the requisite *mens rea* for the offence. (R v Sommani, 2007 BCCA 199 (CanLII))

The document cannot simply be "false" but it must be proven to be "false" in relation to the purpose for which it was created. (R v Benson, 2012 MBCA 94 (CanLII) ("it must be false in relation to the purpose for which it was created"))

"False document" and "forged document" are not interchangable terms. (R v Hawrish, [1986] S.J. No. 846 (C.A.))

Till the investigation now, it can be classified that the documentation was forged.

Uttering vs. Forgery

Uttering forged documents is distinct from making forged documents. The "forgery" is the making of the document, the "uttering" is the use of the document. (R v Wightman, [2003] A.J. No. 1453 (P.C.) ("Forgery deals with the making of the document; uttering deals with the use of the document."))

It could be said that the documentation was created for the misuse of it against the applicant.

CONCLUSION

It can be concluded that the documentation in (exhibit B) has a forged signature of Mr. Horace R. Carby-Samuels and with intent of malicious actions.

EXHIBIT A

me as well as my daughter. Marcella is in the process of completing a Ph.D and lives in Sweden. The Respondent is trying to ruin her reputation as well because he states that he wants to ensure that she will never be able to get a job or to have her name on any collegial research on which she co-operates; and he has made specious reports to her faculty in the process of promoting her expulsion from the Ph.D program. Attached as Exhibit "L" are copies of the numerous postings.

32. I truly believe that the Respondent will continue to bring frivolous actions and use the court system to continue his harassment.

33. I make this Affidavit in support of my Application to have the Respondent found to be a vexatious litigant and for no other or improper purpose.

SWORN BEFORE ME in the City
Of Ottawa, in the Province of Ontario
this 25 day of January 2017.

_____
Horace R. Carby-Samuels

_____
A Commissioner, etc.

Lauren Michelle Dansman, a Commissioner, etc.,
Province of Ontario, while Student-At-Law.
Expires June 16, 2018.

EXHIBIT B

Affidavit of Horace R. Carby-Samuels   Page | 2

5. With respect to the email from Maxine Fielding, I should point out that she lives in New Jersey. I sent her an email on June 1st, 2017 to inquire about Maxine's knowledge of the procedure that I was about to have, given her prior work at hospitals in the United States. Maxine replied to both myself and my daughter on June 3rd, 2017. On June 6th, Marcella communicated the care plan to Maxine in order to assure Maxine that homecare had been arranged successfully for my wife.

6. As I have mentioned in previous Affidavits, I have arranged nursing and personal care by professionals for my wife. She is not being denied access to visitors. Her relatives, friends and neighbours visit regularly without any issues. It is because of Raymond's continued attacks on both myself and my wife and his abusive behaviour towards us that has caused us to not want to see him. As a further example of his attacks, Raymond would regularly call the ambulance services to attend our home suggesting that there was an emergency. I am advised by ambulance services that they have now placed a block on his calls.

7. This recent Motion is yet a further attempt on Raymond to continually attack and abuse us. My wife is well cared for and is mentally competent. We are just tired of the constant abuse by Raymond.

8. I make this Affidavit in support of Raymond's request for an urgent Motion and for no other or improper purpose.

SWORN BEFORE ME in the City
Of Ottawa, in the Province of Ontario   )
this 14 day of September 2017.   )
)   Horace R. Carby-Samuels
)
_____   )
A Commissioner, etc.   )

Zorian Adam Maksymec, a Commissioner, etc.,
Province of Ontario, while Student-At-Law.
Expires March 27, 2020.

EXHIBIT C

22. I make this Affidavit in support of my Motion and for no other or improper purpose.

SWORN BEFORE ME in the City
Of Ottawa, in the Province of Ontario)
this 23rd day of January 2017.)
) _____
) Horace R. Carby-Samuels
)
_____)
A Commissioner, etc.

Lauren Michelle Daneman, a Commissioner, etc.,
Province of Ontario, while Student-At-Law.
Expires June 16, 2019.

5. With respect to the email from Maxine Fielding, I should point out that she lives in New Jersey. I sent her an email on June 1st, 2017 to inquire about Maxine's knowledge of the procedure that I was about to have, given her prior work at hospitals in the United States. Maxine replied to both myself and my daughter on June 3rd, 2017. On June 6th, Marcella communicated the care plan to Maxine in order to assure Maxine that homecare had been arranged successfully for my wife.

6. As I have mentioned in previous Affidavits, I have arranged nursing and personal care by professionals for my wife. She is not being denied access to visitors. Her relatives, friends and neighbours visit regularly without any issues. It is because of Raymond's continued attacks on both myself and my wife and his abusive behaviour towards us that has caused us to not want to see him. As a further example of his attacks, Raymond would regularly call the ambulance services to attend our home suggesting that there was an emergency. I am advised by ambulance services that they have now placed a block on his calls.

7. This recent Motion is yet a further attempt on Raymond to continually attack and abuse us. My wife is well cared for and is mentally competent. We are just tired of the constant abuse by Raymond.

8. I make this Affidavit in support of Raymond's request for an urgent Motion and for no other or improper purpose.

SWORN BEFORE ME in the City
Of Ottawa, in the Province of Ontario
this 14 day of September 2017.

Horace R. Carby-Samuels

A Commissioner, etc.

Zorian Adam Maksymec, a Commissioner, etc.,
Province of Ontario, while Student-At-Law.
Expires March 27, 2020.

Example of apparent deception

www.ingramcontent.com/pod-product-compliance
Lightning Source LLC
Chambersburg PA
CBHW052127110526
44592CB00013B/1783